The Mourner's Book of

Hope

30 Days of Inspiration

ALSO BY ALAN WOLFELT

Eight Critical Questions for Mourners—
And the Answers that Will Help You Heal

Healing A Friend's Grieving Heart: 100 Practical Ideas
for Helping Someone You Love Through Loss

Healing Your Grieving Heart: 100 Practical Ideas

The Journey Through Grief: Reflections on Healing

Living in the Shadow of the Ghosts of Grief:
Step Into the Light

Understanding Your Grief: Ten Essential Touchstones
for Finding Hope and Healing Your Heart

Companion Press is dedicated to the education and support of both the bereaved and bereavement caregivers. We believe that those who companion the bereaved by walking with them as they journey in grief have a wondrous opportunity: to help others embrace and grow through grief—and to lead fuller, more deeply-lived lives themselves because of this important ministry.

For a complete catalog and ordering information, write or call:

Companion Press
The Center for Life and Loss Transition
3735 Broken Bow Road
Fort Collins, Colorado 80526
(970) 226-6050

www.centerforloss.com

The Mourner's Book of

ALAN D. WOLFELT, PH.D.

Companion
PRESS

An imprint of the Center for Loss and Life Transition

Fort Collins, Colorado

Companion Press is an imprint of the Center for Loss and Life Transition, 3735 Broken Bow Road, Fort Collins, Colorado 80526. www.centerforloss.com

Artwork by Christoph Kadur, www.istockphoto.com
Cover design and book layout by Angela P. Hollingsworth

Printed in Canada.

17 16 15 14 13 12 11 10   5 4 3 2 1

ISBN: 978-1-879651-65-4

Introduction

Today...
I open my heart's hand to allow...
the touch of hope.

~ Julia Cameron

Someone you love has died. In your heart you have come to know your deepest pain. Your grief has brought challenges that seem beyond your own capacity to survive. Grief creates chaos, and your soul cries out. You naturally experience a sense of helplessness and, at times, you feel the depths of hopelessness. It all feels so incredibly overwhelming. And as you live in this painful place, you come to learn that you must surrender to your grief, sit in your wound, and make space for your lost self.

If your experience is in any way like my own and those of the thousands of mourners I have had the honor to walk with and learn from, you are feeling abandoned and alone right now. You may instinctively be questioning the meaning and purpose of life. You recognize that so many things in your daily life have changed—your plans, your dreams, your concerns, and your roles. You may discover yourself searching for a reason to go on living in the face of this loss and asking countless "How?" and "Why?" questions.

"How can this be happening?"
"How am I going to make it through this?"
"Why did this happen now, in this way?"
"Why am I feeling so lost?"

When we experience a loss—whether it is the death of someone loved, a divorce loss, the loss of a job, or a significant change in health—loss reminds us of how little control we really have over some things about life and living. Naturally, these kinds of losses (among many others) can leave us feeling incredibly powerless, seemingly helpless, and deeply hopeless at times.

When we lose someone we love, it changes us. The person who died was a part of you and part of your life. This death means you must mourn a loss not only outside yourself, but inside yourself as well. At times, overwhelming sadness and loneliness may be constant companions to you on this grief journey. You may feel that when this person died, part of you died with him or her. And now you are faced with finding some sense of meaning at a time when you may be feeling empty and alone.

Your loneliness and emptiness are often present, even when you are in the midst of family and friends. When others try to help by saying, "I know just how you feel," they usually do not. They cannot. They are not walking this walk for you. Your pain, your questions, your doubts, and your fears are unique. No one can know exactly how this feels for you.

While your grief is unique, some of the questions you may be asking are universal. The fears, doubts, and questions that come when we experience grief have been with us since the beginning of our awareness that loss is part of the cycle of life. Loss truly is an integral part of life. You are asking questions that others before you have raised. Questions that have been raised *to* God. Questions that have been asked *about* God. Like others who have been where you are, you may be feeling distant from God, perhaps even questioning the existence of God. These kinds of questions have been preserved in time because they belong to and are asked by most everyone who experiences the pain of loss.

So, like your fellow travelers on this grief journey, you are faced with sitting in the wound of your grief. When you sit in the wound of your grief, you surrender to it in recognition that the only way to the other side of the pain and hopelessness is *through* the pain and hopelessness. You acknowledge that you are willing to do the work that mourning requires. Paradoxically, it is in befriending your wound that eventually you will restore your life and reinvest in living.

Loss of Your Divine Spark and the Role of Hope in Your Healing

People in grief often come to see me on the sacred grounds of the Center for Loss and Life Transition. When they begin their grief journey, they often start by expressing their sense of hopelessness by saying, "I feel so hopeless," or, "I am not sure I can go on living." Like you, the losses that have touched their lives have naturally muted, if not extinguished, their *divine spark*. Their divine spark is that internal energy that gives meaning and purpose to life. Your divine spark or life force is the keeper of your mind, your body, and your soul.

I discovered some time ago that a central part of my helping role is to gently and quietly bring hope to those in grief. Hope that encourages them to discover a renewed divine spark and a desire to reenter life with meaning and purpose. Each and every one of us as humans has a divine spark. We are each the keeper of our own spark or life force. My personal life losses and my role as a caregiver to others have taught me that hope is the vital ingredient that helps us reignite our divine spark after loss breaks our hearts and touches our souls.

The more I reflected on the role of hope in healing from life losses, the more compelled I was to write a user-friendly, easy-to-read book that would help mourners invite hope into their lives. This book

Hopelessness and Depression

Before I go any further, I must clarify the difference between the natural, intermittent hopelessness that mourners often feel and the unyielding hopelessness that is depression. **If you are experiencing grief that is so debilitating and severe that you cannot function or that is causing you to entertain thoughts of suicide, please get professional help right away.** A trained grief counselor will be able to determine if you are clinically depressed and get you started on a path toward healing, which might include therapy and antidepressant medication. Once your depression has softened some, you will be ready and able to embrace the hope that is the subject of this book. In fact, seeking professional help is the first step on the road to hope because it indicates that you are hopeful that your life can and will be better. Remember, seeking the help you need is not a sign of weakness, it is a sign of strength!

of hope is anchored in reflections and my favorite quotes on the role of hope in healing. Because quotes often capture the essence of certain life experience, I've included many throughout this book for you to reflect on when you need to be reminded of the importance of hope. This book invites you to find and experience the hope that you will need to slowly, over time, and with no reward for speed, mourn well so that you can go on to live well and love well. My wish for you is that these pages help you nurture your divine spark back toward light and life. This book, directed from my heart to your heart, is an invitation to come out of the dark and into the light.

Each day you will discover several quotes to meditate on that, when read slowly and thoughtfully, will help you befriend hope and rediscover meaning and purpose in your life. Review the reflections and quotes in this little book of comfort and hope and embrace the ones that resonate with you. Then revisit them from time to time as you take them into your heart. When you find you are doubting yourself or your journey, read the words that speak to you as a way of nurturing yourself back toward life and living. These enduring and wise observations from some of the world's greatest hope-filled philosophers will help you to begin reprogramming your attitude and your view of the world around you.

My hope is that you find this little book to be a gentle companion that gives you wisdom and strength for today, tomorrow, and each day that follows.

My Prayer For You

May you continue to discover hope. May you continue to find new ways to renew your divine spark and to believe that meaning, purpose, and love will come back into your life. No, you did not go in search of this loss. But it has come to you, and you have discovered the importance of sitting in your wound on the pathway to your healing. If you give up, the essence of who you are will die or be muted for the rest of your life. Hope can and will keep this from happening.

May you never give up and may you consciously choose life! May you turn your face to the radiance of joy every day. May you live in the continued awareness that you are being cradled in love by a caring presence that never deserts you. May you keep your heart open wide and receptive to what life brings you, both happy and sad. And may you walk a pathway to living your life fully and on purpose until you die.

Blessings to you as you befriend hope and choose to celebrate life. May your divine spark shine brightly as you share your gifts and your love with the universe.

I sincerely hope we have the chance to meet one day!

Alan D. Wolfelt

Day 1

Know That You Will Survive

Beginnings are scary. Endings are usually sad, but it's what's in the middle that counts. So, when you find yourself at the beginning, just give hope a chance to float up. And it will!

~ Hope Floats

It may be difficult for you to believe right now, but you will survive this. I know that you will survive because we all have the capacity to mourn in ways that integrate loss into our lives. Just as a physical wound on your body heals when you give it proper care and attention, when you take time to care for and attend to the painful emotional and spiritual wounds that are present in your life, you will find hope and healing.

Let yourself whisper these hope-filled words, "I will survive." Take the words in and just hold them in your mind and heart for a moment. They are there to offer reassurance when you question whether or not you can keep going. Let these words carry you through the next breath, the next moment, the next hour, the next day, for as long as you need to be carried.

One way to bring hope into your life right now is to gently remind yourself that you will survive somehow, someway. You don't have to know exactly how or why or when, but know that you will make it through to the other side of this. Begin each day by reminding yourself that you will survive. Gently remind yourself …

- *The future is going to feel brighter because the darkness will soften as I move through my grief;*
- *These raw emotions that I'm feeling right now will lessen as long as I allow myself to feel the pain when is surfaces; and*

I find hope in the darkest of days, and focus in the brightest. I do not judge the universe.

~ Dalai Lama

- *I will not always feel this way because each of us has the capacity to heal. I have the capacity to befriend my grief and integrate this profound loss into my life.*

Gently bring hope for survival into your life each day. As you do this, your broken heart will begin to heal. Your healed heart will be able to feel love, joy, and happiness again. Your mind will find some of the answers it is seeking, and those answers will be enough. You can gather enough energy to get through the next hour or day, and that energy will be a gentle reminder that your divine spark is preparing to be reignited.

Let hope in somehow, somewhere…and believe that you will survive.

When the world says, "Give up," Hope whispers, "Try it one more time."

~ Unknown

Personal Reflection on Hope

How will I remind myself each day that I WILL survive this?

_____

_____

_____

_____

_____

_____

_____

_____

_____

_____

_____

_____

_____

_____

_____

_____

_____

Day 2

Keep Your Heart Open

The inability to open up to hope is what blocks trust,
and blocked trust is the reason for blighted dreams.

~ Elizabeth Gilbert

Naturally, it may be difficult for you to open your heart right now. Your heart may be so filled with pain that opening it feels impossible. But living with an open heart is one way to allow hope to come into your life.

When someone we love dies, our heart and mind are initially flooded with emotion. We cannot believe that the person we love will not physically be part of our everyday life any longer. At times the hurt runs so deep that we want to put up walls and protect our vulnerable heart.

We want to protect our heart from being flooded. Because we are so overwhelmed with grief, it feels as if there is no room to take in anything more. We are vulnerable, and we naturally want to protect our heart from feeling any more loss or pain. When someone we love dies, we often fear losing more things that are precious to us.

Protecting your heart by taking care of yourself is one of the best things you can do for yourself when you are grieving the death of someone loved. Eating well, exercising, and getting enough rest are among the ways you can take care of yourself right now.

Protecting your heart by retreating from the support and love of others, on the other hand, is not something that will help you heal. Your body, mind, and emotional self may want to build walls and guard against loving and receiving love from others right now. Holding love at arm's length means you may be

Love comes to those who still hope even though they've been disappointed, to those who still believe even though they've been betrayed, to those who still love even though they've been hurt before.

~ Unknown

missing out on the opportunity to have loving support, genuine caring, and authentic warmth at a time when you need them the most.

Perhaps it is helpful to remind yourself that your heart is your "well of reception." It is moved entirely by what it has perceived. Authentic mourning is an opportunity to embrace your open heart in ways that allow for and encourage your eventual healing.

This loss is a reminder that love is precious. It is something you want to experience as much and as often as possible. Love never dies. Even the love you feel for the person who died still exists. Over time you will transform that love into loving memory and carry it with you for the rest of your life.

Don't turn away from the support or love others have to offer, even in the face of fear. Keep your heart open to love, and hope will find its way in, no matter how overwhelmed by grief you may feel.

To love is to risk not being loved in return. To hope is to risk pain. To try is to risk failure, but risk must be taken because the greatest hazard in life is to risk nothing.
~ Unknown

Personal Reflection on Hope

Is my heart open or closed right now? What am I doing to keep my heart open to love in the face of this painful loss?

_____

_____

_____

_____

_____

_____

_____

_____

_____

_____

_____

_____

_____

Day 3

Befriend Hope

If children have the ability to ignore all odds and percentages, then maybe we can all learn from them. When you think about it, what other choice is there but to hope? We have two options, medically and emotionally: give up, or Fight Like Hell.

~ Lance Armstrong

What is hope? It is an expectation of a good that is yet to be. It is an inner knowing that the future holds positive things. It is trust that no matter the current circumstances, the days to come will reveal a renewed capacity to allow joy and happiness into your soul.

Befriending hope will lift your spirits. To befriend literally means you are making an effort to "become friends" with hope. Imagine what it would be like to have hope as a friend rather than a distant relative or a partner that you have lost touch with.

We often do not think of hope as something concrete, so you may question whether or not it's even possible to really befriend it. I assure you it is, and it is an important part of your healing process to find ways to make friends with it. When we are encountering a difficult life loss, we need friends and constant companions to help us through. Hope can be one of your compassionate companions on this journey.

Befriending hope is no different than what you've done to cultivate other relationships in your life. You cultivate a relationship with hope by believing it has value, making time for it, and spending time nurturing and maintaining it by communicating with it on a regular basis. If it will help you, you can make hope something concrete; let something physical represent hope as you develop your relationship with it. What represents hope for you? It can be a hope rock that you carry

Hope is like a road in the country; there was never a road, but when many people walk on it, the road comes into existence.

~ Lin Yutang

with you. It can be the flowers you plant in your garden and spend time with each weekend caring for and communing with. Hope can be found in this book that you sit with each night before you go to sleep. It can be a quote, a photo, or a song that touches you deeply. It can be a sanctuary you enjoy or an activity like driving in the mountains or a place you are able to sit quietly with hope.

Find something that resonates with you and use it to help you begin the process of inviting hope into your life and befriending it with open arms. Whatever you choose, let it be something that when you see it, hear it, touch it, or sit with it… it is hope for you.

Hope is the dream of a waking man.
~ Aristotle

The present is the ever-moving shadow that divides yesterday from tomorrow. In that lies hope.
~ Frank Lloyd Wright

Personal Reflection on Hope

In what specific ways am I befriending hope? Set a time to meet a friend to explore the role that hope is playing in your transformative journey.

_____

_____

_____

_____

_____

_____

_____

_____

_____

_____

_____

_____

Day 4

Understand That Time Does Not Heal All Wounds

Hope is like the sun, which, as we journey toward it, casts the shadow of our burden behind us.

~ Samuel Smiles

Throughout this journey, others will do their best to offer comfort and support to you. Even the most caring people may turn to you during this time and say things like, *"Don't worry, in time you'll feel better"* and *"You'll get through this in time"* or the classic cliché, *"Time heals all wounds."* Though these words are uttered with the best of intentions, they are platitudes or trite expressions, offered as hope and reassurance that the pain of grief will subside...in time.

The pain and hurt you carry right now will not last forever, that is true. But it's not the amount of time that goes by that will bring hope and heal your grieving heart. In order for you to authentically heal from this loss, you must find ways to integrate the loss into your life. Time alone does not lead to healing. In reality, grief waits on welcome, not on time.

It is what you DO with the time you have and with the pain that surfaces that will inspire hope, healing, and transformation in your life. As you allow yourself to feel the pain in small ways then allow it to retreat until you are ready for the next wave (feel your grief in "doses"), giving yourself permission to search for meaning, you will integrate this loss and reconcile it into your life. To reconcile is to experience a renewed sense of energy and confidence, an ability to fully acknowledge the reality of the death, and a capacity to become reenrolled in the activities of living.

Hope is a renewable option: If you run out of it at the end of the day, you get to start over in the morning.

~ Barbara Kingsolver

You will slowly, with no rewards for speed, come to reconcile your grief. Beyond an intellectual working through of the death, there is also an emotional and spiritual working through. What has been understood in your "head" will be joined by your "heart."

Remember, time will not heal your wound. What you actively do with your grief over time is what will bring hope and healing to you.

Hope is not a feeling; it is something you do.
~ Katherine Paterson

Were it not for hope, the heart would break.
~ Scottish Proverb

Personal Reflection on Hope

How am I using my time to actively integrate this loss into my life?

_____

_____

_____

_____

_____

_____

_____

_____

_____

_____

_____

_____

_____

Day 5

Ask Questions

Remember the brown leaf falling with certainty from the tallest of trees. Hope is the wind that catches it, carries it, tenders it and finally delivers it to rest beside the acorn.

~ David Bailey

We never know how high we are till we are called to rise; and then, if we are true to plan, our statures touch the sky.

~ Emily Dickinson

Asking questions is an important part of your grief journey. Thoughts and beliefs that you've carried with you your entire lifetime may now be in question. Death makes us question beliefs that have helped us to feel safe, secure, and steady as we walked through the world. Part of our grief work involves redefining certain aspects of our selves and our ways of being in the world.

You go through this redefining of things because some of your long-held beliefs no longer fit into your experience in the world. For example, you may have always felt that "life is fair," but this unfair death has you questioning this truism. Perhaps you have always believed that you can handle anything that comes your way, but coping with this situation feels unbearable at times. You may be questioning long-held beliefs or commitments to the religion that you've practiced since you were a child. As you think about the inevitability of death, you may find yourself questioning the meaning and purpose of your own life.

At times, you may feel stuck in a dark place of sadness with no way out. Life is drained of its meaning, and you may be feeling dispirited and joyless. You may feel abandoned in a world full of chaos and confusion. You may question if laughter will ever again be possible. The turmoil reflected in your instinctive questions is anchored in spiritual pain. You have been uprooted from what is comfortable and familiar in your everyday life. You are surrounded by unknowns that naturally elicit questions as you strive to discover new patterns in your

I must encounter my questions, my doubts, my fears.
There is richness in these domains. As I explore them,
I don't reinforce my tensions but instead release them.
In this way, I transcend my grief and discover new life
beyond anything my heart could ever have comprehended.

~ Alan D. Wolfelt

Learn from yesterday, live for today, hope for tomorrow.
The important thing is to not stop questioning

~ Albert Einstein

life. Your questions are part of your struggle to come to terms with what has happened to you.

Don't believe the advice that others may give you about questions: "You will never find the answers, so there is no point in asking the questions." Your questions are important right now. They bring you hope that it is possible to grow through grief. Questions are necessary in helping you discover how you are going to look at the world, at relationships, and at yourself from this point forward. They are an opportunity to look more closely at the way you are living and the way you want to live the rest of your life.

Take this opportunity to question and redefine your life. You are undergoing a transformation right now, and part of this involves establishing a set of beliefs that help you operate and function well in the world. A new you is unfolding, and asking questions is an important part of that unfolding process. Allow yourself to ponder questions that will help you grow and develop a deeper understanding of how you want your life to be from here forward. Consider the following questions as a way to help you work on redefining certain aspects of yourself and your life right now:

Why did this happen?

Why now? Why this way?

What does my future hold?

What is important to me?

Am I spending my time doing things that are important to me in the company of people I love?

Do the people in my life know that I love them?

Why am I here? What is my purpose?

Is my life fulfilling?

When life feels unfair, how do I handle it? How do I want to handle it?

Personal Reflection on Hope

What are my most pressing questions as I encounter this journey into grief? Who can sit and be present to me in ways that support my need to explore these questions?

_____

_____

_____

_____

_____

Day 6

Consciously Choose Hope

Hope is always available to us. When we feel defeated, we need only take a deep breath and say, "Yes," and hope will reappear.

~ Monroe Forester

Hope is not something that will just passively float into your life. Instead, hope will enter when you create ways to consciously bring it into your day. Just as we all have the capacity to heal, we all have the capacity to choose hope and to consciously cultivate it at any given moment. The door you open to hope each day will dramatically influence the quality of the life you live.

Consciously cultivating hope means deliberately focusing on it —paying attention to it, inviting it into a given moment and letting yourself feel it as it enters. You can consciously choose to focus on hope any time you desire. There are countless ways to consciously cultivate and choose hope.

Here are a few ideas to consider:

- *Write the word "hope." Place the word somewhere that is visible to you (such as your mirror, to remind you of the importance of giving hope your attention).*

- *Carry or wear something that has the word "hope" on it—a hope rock, a keychain, or a piece of jewelry, for example.*

- *Surround yourself with others who are hope-filled rather than those who are hope-deprived or are experiencing hopelessness related to things going on in their own lives.*

- *Sit and quietly focus your attention on something that represents hope to you—a candle, a quote, or a photograph of something hopeful, for example.*

Hope doesn't come from calculating whether the good news is winning out over the bad. It's simply a choice to take action.

~ Anna Lappé

Hope costs nothing.

~ Colette

- *Embrace the preciousness of each moment. Loss and grief teach you the importance of living in the present moment. The here and now is the resting place of your heart and soul. In the present moment comes the rebirth of hope and the meaning of the life you search for. You surrender to what you have lost and begin anew.*

- *Sit in stillness and allow yourself to experience the presence of God. Cultivate His presence in your life, every day, every hour, every moment.*

- *Find a sacred space that feels hope-filled and visit it frequently.*

- *Make a collage of words or pictures that symbolize hope in your mind and heart.*

Be creative with how you consciously give attention to hope and invite it in. On a daily basis, choose hope over emptiness. Choose hope rather than doubt. Choose hope instead of despair. When you are feeling empty, doubtful, or hopeless, consciously choose to bring hope to that moment.

Hope and hopelessness are both choices. Why not choose hope?

~ Greg Anderson

Personal Reflection on Hope

What are some of the ways I have chosen or will consciously choose to focus on hope each day?

_____

_____

_____

_____

_____

_____

_____

_____

_____

_____

_____

_____

_____

_____

_____

Day 7

Sit in the Quietness of Hope

Hope is grief's best music.

~ Anonymous

Hope is a state of mind, not of the world. Hope, in this deep and powerful sense, is not the same as joy that things are going well, or willingness to invest in enterprises that are obviously heading for success, but rather an ability to work for something because it is good.

~ Václav Havel

Though hope can be found in sounds, it can also be experienced in moments of quiet, when silence enters the room. Where there is silence, there is an opportunity to sit in the quietness of hope. Sitting in the quietness of hope is a peaceful way to allow it to join you in a particular moment or experience.

In silent moments, hope is in your breath. It is part of every meditation you do. Hope is in your body's stretch. It is part of each yoga pose. Hope is in the flicker of a newly lit candle. It is part of every silent ritual you perform. Hope is in the steps you take. It is part of every walk or hike you make. It is part of every silent drive you take. Hope is in the comfort of the chair you sit in. It is part of every moment you sit in contemplation on your porch or deck, at your desk, in your living room, or anyplace that you choose.

You can recognize hope is present when you feel the calm, the relaxation that fills you as you sit in quietness. The quietness reminds you that calm is something that you can find anytime, anywhere. All you need to do is to find a pocket of quiet to experience it. In every quiet moment is the opportunity to connect with hope through calm.

The next time you are in a silent space or you intentionally find a spot of quiet to sit in, breathe in and out and wait. Calm will enter that moment. There is no need to say or do anything as you sit in the quietness. Just simply, in your mind and heart, whisper, "Hope…I can feel you. You are here." Hope is with you in this moment of silent presence. Just be with hope; sit and share the quietness together.

Personal Reflection on Hope

Find a place that quiets your spirit. Take this meditative journal with you. Sit in stillness for ten full minutes and begin to write below and see what comes up for you.

_____

_____

_____

_____

_____

_____

_____

_____

_____

_____

Sitting in the quietness of hope encourages me to
discover so many reasons to live fully until I die.
~ Alan D. Wolfelt

Day 8

Move Toward Your Pain

Hope is a song in a weary throat.

~ Pauli Murray

The death of someone loved can be one of the most difficult life experiences we go through as human beings. Loss brings uninvited pain into our lives. The heart is tender during grief and, at times, the depth of the pain is indescribable.

A tender heart needs attention and nurturance. Your tender heart needs to be cared for right now, and caring means that you give some attention to the pain you are experiencing. There is hope … you will not always feel this tender, and this loss will not always feel so overwhelmingly painful.

We are creatures who naturally want to prevent, avoid, or move away from pain, though. In doing so, we only prolong our suffering. Moving away from pain prevents you from feeling it, working through it, and integrating it into your being. By not allowing yourself to move toward the pain of this loss, you will risk carrying it with you into tomorrow, into next year, and for years into your future.

The reality is that integrating grief into your life requires commitment and intention if you are to become whole again. Commitment goes hand in hand with the concept of "setting your intention." Intention is defined as *being conscious of what you want to experience.*

This concept of intention-setting presupposes that your outer reality is a direct reflection of your inner thoughts, beliefs, and hopes. If you can choose to mold some of your thoughts and beliefs, then you can influence your hopes. Of course, you will

When we become aware that we do not have to escape our pains, but that we can mobilize them into a common search for life, those very pains are transformed from expressions of despair into signs of hope.

~ Henri Nouwen

Hope is the dream of a soul awake.

~ French Proverb

have to honor and embrace your pain because a guiding truth, which Helen Keller taught us years ago, is that "the only way to the other side is through."

Carried grief is heavy, and it can weigh down so many aspects of life. The weight of carried grief mutes your divine spark until you move through it and reach the other side of it. Moving toward your grief means allowing yourself to experience the pain of your loss in doses and to express that pain outwardly (at times in the presence of supportive others and at times alone).

As you move toward your pain, you will be leaving a path for hope to enter your tender heart. As hope enters your heart, you will be filled with the promise and possibility of walking into your future without carrying grief with you.

We must always have old memories and young hopes.

~ Arsene Houssaye

Personal Reflection on Hope

How are you moving toward your pain rather than away from it?

_____

_____

_____

_____

_____

_____

_____

_____

_____

_____

_____

_____

_____

_____

Day 9

Borrow Hope If You Need To

Hope is the feeling you have that the feeling you have isn't permanent.

~ Jean Kerr

At times your sadness might run so deep that you cannot even imagine what having hope would feel like. Your heart feels broken. Your divine spark is subdued by grief. You may question, at times, how and if you are going to make it through this. These are the moments when cultivating hope seems impossible. Hope seems so remote.

If hope feels out of reach right now, consider borrowing a little to get you through. When you cannot muster the energy to cultivate it yourself, it's possible to receive hope from others. It's okay in times like these to turn to people who have hope to lend.

This loss has affected you deeply. Right now, inviting people into your life who carry hope is important. Spending time with compassionate others who are hope-filled rather than hope-depleted can help you through some of your most sorrowful moments.

How do you know someone is hope-filled? These are friends or family members who have a hopeful outlook on life. They are caring, non-judgmental listeners. They are people who have a positive energy when you are in their presence, and they make you smile just simply by being around them.

While you may wish everyone you know could be a support to you, keep in mind my "rule of thirds." One-third of people are usually neutral; they don't help you or hurt you. One-third are harmful and end up making you feel worse than you did

Hope is the pillar that holds up the world.

~ Anonymous

*A very small degree of hope is sufficient
to cause the birth of love.*

~ Stendhal

before you were in their presence. And one-third will be your empathetic, hope-filled companions. Seek out your friends and family in this last group.

Although these companions cannot physically give you hope, the energy they radiate can anchor you right now. This vicarious experience with hope may be necessary when your supply is running low or you lack the energy to actively cultivate hope yourself. Borrow enough to sustain you for now and plan more time with them when you know you may need more.

Hope is a renewable resource...borrow it now and know that in the future, when you are less depleted, you may be paying it forward to someone else in need.

Hope is the thing with feathers, that perches in the soul, and sings the tune without words, and never stops at all.

~ Emily Dickinson

Personal Reflection On Hope

Who are the people in my life who are hope-filled? Who will I
call when I need to borrow a little hope to get me through?

_____

_____

_____

_____

_____

_____

_____

_____

_____

_____

_____

_____

_____

_____

_____

Day 10

Know That There Are No Rewards for Speed

One of the realities of grief and loss is that the rest of the world seems to keep going forward, while you feel you have been stopped in your tracks. So, stop, look, listen, and reach out for hope. Then and only then will you discover movement in your quest to rediscover meaning and purpose in life.

~ Alan D. Wolfelt

When someone you love dies, it can feel as if the world stops. You feel as if you are standing still or moving in slow motion. Feelings of shock, numbness, and disbelief are helping you to slow down so that you can take in the most difficult news a human being can be given—someone has died. These feelings are your body and mind's way of protecting you early in the grief process.

But as you begin to return to your daily routine, as you may have already, you discover the world never actually stopped. The pace of the world didn't slow down even the slightest. The daily triumphs and tribulations of family and friends continued. Their lives went on as usual despite the death and despite your life coming to a halt.

And now you are faced with the pressure of getting back up to normal speed again. You may be pressuring yourself, or you may have others insisting, that you "get back to normal." The problem is that "normal" doesn't exist any longer for you, because part of grief involves establishing a new sense of normal. And what is considered normal speed in the hurried world we live in today is much faster than you may be ready to move.

As you move through grief, keep in mind that moving fast is not always better. Though you may be receiving consistent messages from others (or perhaps even yourself) about the need to "get over" your grief and get on with your life, gently tell

All human wisdom is summed up in two words: wait and hope.

~ Alexandre Dumas

Every area of trouble gives out a ray of hope; and the one unchangeable certainty is that nothing is certain or unchangeable.

~ John Fitzgerald Kennedy

yourself there are no rewards for speed when it comes to grief. That's right: There are no rewards for speed.

In part, others encourage you to speed through your grief out of their own sense of helplessness and discomfort with grief. They desperately want to reduce the pain you feel, which is impossible, so they encourage you to act as if it's not there. This only creates the illusion that you are free of it, because grief remains despite any attempts to suppress or ignore it. In fact, in some ways it gives grief permission to stick around and fester, because you are not giving it the attention it needs to soften.

Even the most compassionate others may not understand the role of pain in grief and the importance of allowing you to sit in the wound as you move toward hope and healing. The more others push and you listen, the faster you will feel you have to "get over" or "let go" of your grief. Yet the faster you try to make it happen, the longer it will take. Fast, rushed, hurried movements do not allow you to experience your thoughts and emotions fully or to express them across time as you do the work of mourning.

Remind yourself that this journey is not about "getting over" your grief. Rather, it is a journey that helps you to reconcile and integrate all that has changed in you and in your world. Walking—deliberately, consciously, intentionally—through grief helps you give this loss a little space in your heart to reside so that it does not consume you every moment of every day. Remind yourself that despite what others are recommending, there are no rewards for speed when it comes to grief work.

Personal Reflection on Hope

What can I do to remind myself there are no rewards for speed during my grief journey.?

_____

_____

_____

_____

_____

_____

_____

_____

_____

_____

Day 11

Share Your Story

The message of hope never grows old.
It's the greatest story that ever was told.
It's the green in the grass and the blue in the sky.
It's the reason we have the courage to try.

~ song lyrics by David Bailey

If the pain of your grief feels overwhelming, you are not alone. The thoughts and feelings that come when someone we love dies feel heavy and overpowering sometimes. It may feel as if no one could possibly understand how this truly feels for you.

No one else can understand your experience fully because they are not you. Your grief journey is unique and personal. Although even the most compassionate person cannot completely comprehend what this is like for you, you can find comfort and hope when you surround yourself with people who will honor your story of this loss.

Sharing your story with those who have the capacity to bear witness to what this experience is like through your eyes and in your heart can be a hope-filled, healing experience. Give someone the opportunity to walk with you in the wilderness by teaching him or her about the loss of this precious person in your life.

Expressing what this experience is like for you is one way to release the pain that has permeated your heart and to mourn this devastating loss. Sharing will bring you hope because it will allow you to feel heard, understood, and loved. The creation of new meaning and purpose in life requires that you "re-story" your life.

Find others who truly listen—others who let you share without trying to fix, take away, or distract you from what you are feeling. If telling your story is difficult for you, take time to write it out

Hope rallies energies and activates the commitment to authentically mourn in ways that relight your divine spark.

~ Alan D. Wolfelt

Hope soothes, rallies, and creates survivors.

~ Nancy Fusillo

and share it with someone. Consider drawing something that represents what this grief journey feels like and communicate your story through pictures instead of words with someone who is able to simply take in what you are saying. Share your story in whatever way feels most natural to you.

Because stories of love and loss take time, patience, and unconditional love, they serve as powerful antidotes to a modern society that is all too often preoccupied with getting you to "let go," "move on," and "have closure." Whether it be a friend, a family member, a counselor, or someone who is a fellow traveler in grief whom you've met through a support group, having others honor your story is one way to invite hope into your journey and to continue this process of healing.

Hope is a universal language.

~ Unknown

Personal Reflection on Hope

Who is one person with whom you can share your story this week? Where are the places in which it feels safe to share your story, where you know that you will be heard and not encouraged to move away from the pain of your grief?

_____

_____

_____

_____

_____

_____

_____

_____

_____

_____

_____

_____

_____

_____

_____

Day 12

Don't Just Grieve, Mourn

Most of the important things in the world have been accomplished by people who have kept on trying when there seemed to be no hope at all.

~ Dale Carnegie

Everything that is done in the world is done by hope.

~ Martin Luther

The death of someone loved has brought unimaginable pain into your life. Though your heart is breaking, it will heal as you allow yourself to mourn this difficult loss. As you continue this journey, you will find hope in mourning. This comes when you realize you have the capacity to actively transform your grief by openly mourning this loss.

Grief and mourning are often talked about interchangeably, but they are not the same. Your *grief* is the compilation of thoughts and feelings that welled up within you when you first encountered this painful loss and that remain inside you as you cope with the changes that this loss has brought into your life. *Mourning* is when you actively participate in taking your grief from the inside to the outside, expressing these painful thoughts and feelings outside of yourself.

Authentic mourning means being consciously aware of the painful emotions of grief and feeling safe to express them. This may seem odd because your initial response following loss is instinctive and organic. The loss has taken place, and you naturally feel core feelings such as helplessness, anxiety, fear, despair, protest, and sadness.

Herein lies the paradox—a wide range of instinctive responses occur, but you get to decide as your grief unfolds into mourning if you will truly experience these responses or instead inhibit, suppress, or deny them. Actually, befriending such emotions is what makes it possible to eventually experience a sense of

There is no hope unmingled with fear,
and no fear unmingled with hope.

~ Baruch Spinoza

If you lose hope, somehow you lose the vitality
that keeps life moving, you lose that courage to be,
that quality that helps you go on despite it all.

~ Martin Luther King

renewed meaning and purpose in your life. Interestingly, the emotions you most want to avoid are the ones you most need to attend to. Somewhere in the collision between the heart, which searches for permanency and connection, and the brain, which acknowledges separation and loss, there is a need for all of us to authentically mourn.

Don't just grieve this loss; experience the hope that comes with allowing yourself to mourn it as well. If you choose only to grieve, you will allow that pain to seep into your soul and you will carry it with you into your day, into your work, into your home, and into your relationships with others. Instead, find healthy ways to openly transform your grief into mourning. Feeling it is the only way to heal the wound.

Find ways to release your grief and express what you are feeling outside of yourself. There are countless ways to experience the hope that comes when you allow yourself to mourn—write, draw, find music that moves you, wear black, scrapbook photos of the person who died, watch a movie that encourages emotion to surface, share your story about the death with a compassionate listener, spend time where the person you love is memorialized, display photographs that help you remember the person who died, light a candle for the person who died. Whatever you chose to do, know that you are cultivating hope even as you do the work of mourning.

Personal Reflection on Hope

In what ways am I moving this grief that I feel inside to the outside and openly mourning this loss?

_____

_____

_____

_____

_____

_____

_____

_____

_____

_____

_____

_____

_____

_____

Day 13

Slow Down

You have to have emptiness before it can be filled.
You have to exhale before you can inhale.

~ Tom Yeomans

There may be days when you don't even feel like getting out of bed because the weight of your grief feels too heavy or cumbersome. It may feel as if grief is weighing you down. In some respects, grief does intentionally weigh us down.

The weight of grief is a reminder to you that what your body and soul need most right now is to slow down, stop, rest, and just be. The sluggishness and fatigue you may be feeling are your body's way of saying, "DO less and BE more." The disorganization and short-term memory loss you may be experiencing are your mind's way of telling you, "THINK less and FEEL more." The endless questions and inability to comprehend this reality may be your spirit's way of shouting, "WORK less and LIVE more."

Hope has a hard time catching up with you when you are trying to move fast and keep busy through grief. Hope finds you when you take it slowly, let yourself experience the full reality of this loss, and find ways to integrate it into your being physically, intellectually, emotionally, and spiritually.

During this difficult time, tell yourself that it is okay to slow down, to not do so much, and to allow yourself to rest and go into neutral for at least a little while. Listen to your body, your mind, and your spirit begging you to lighten your load.

It's hard in our culture to allow ourselves to slow down and just be in the moment with our grief. We more naturally want to run away from it, but grief will follow us. It seems easier

Hope never abandons you, you abandon it.

~ George Weinberg

at times to just put it up and away on a shelf, but grief will remain on that emotional shelf until we decide to open it and really experience it fully. When we shelve our grief, it weighs us down, making us less emotionally available because it's taking up space.

Lighten your load today and slow down so that hope can catch up to you. If you choose not to slow down, your grief will continue to beg for your attention and slow you down anyway. Listen to your body and soul; slow down long enough to be with your grief and give it the attention it deserves today.

What oxygen is to the lungs, such is hope to the meaning of life.

~ Emil Brunner

Personal Reflection on Hope

What messages are my body, mind, and heart sending me that are reminding me to slow down and be with my grief? Am I resistant to a slower pace, and if so, what can I do to consciously attend to my need to walk and not run through my grief?

_____

_____

_____

_____

_____

_____

_____

_____

_____

_____

_____

_____

Day 14

Come Back to the Present Moment

Hope is important because it can make the present moment less difficult to bear. If we believe that tomorrow will be better, we can bear a hardship today.

~ Thich Nhat Hanh

Hope is some extraordinary spiritual grace that God gives us to control our fears, not to oust them.

~ Anonymous

Hope can always be found in the present moment. So often, however, we are not in the present moment. Hope is an expectation of a good that is yet to come. The expectation is something that you possess right now, in the present moment.

All you have is this moment. The present moment is rich, and living outside the moment means you are missing out on experiencing what is right in front of you. If you are a parent, that means moments in which your children are trying to connect with you. If you are a spouse, that means moments of feeling nurtured by another. If you have brothers or sisters, that means missed opportunities to connect with your family members who are still physically here to share their stories, their hugs, and their wisdom.

When the present moment is so filled with heartache, it is natural to want to move away from it. It may block the pain when you ruminate about the past, numb yourself in the present, or worry about the future. Detaching from the present may mean that you are detaching from your grief. Doing this in doses in normal, but detaching and avoiding the present emotions is not the pathway toward healing.

It is natural as part of your grief journey to spend time on the past, to remember the person you loved so much who is no longer physically present to you. You may be asking questions to try to find something that will help you makes sense of what happened in the past; "Why our family?" "Why this

For when hope does awaken, an entire life awakens along with it. One comes fully to life.

~ John S. Dunne

Life without hope during times of grief and loss is a life without meaning and purpose.

~ Alan D. Wolfelt

way?" "Why now?" "Why me?" Spending time reflecting on questions about the past is a normal and necessary part of your grief journey. Those who do not question do not find. It is also natural to spend time and give attention to what lies ahead right now. You may feel worried about the future or long for the day you will feel better.

Be observant and notice. If you are spending too much time in the past—or in the future—during this grief journey, you risk neglecting what could be bringing light into your life right now. If you are able to bring yourself into the present moment, you will not miss seeing, hearing, and touching the things that are right in front of you that inspire hope and will help you heal. Practice bringing yourself back to the present moment throughout the day. Focus on what resides in the present moment with you—your breath, the physical signals your body is giving you, noticing what is in the space that surrounds you, or giving attention to the people who are right in front of you. These are examples of where hope lies in the present moment.

Personal Reflection on Hope

Am I living in the present moment? What will I do to bring myself back to the present moment when I find that I am preoccupied with the past or worried about the future?

_____

_____

_____

_____

_____

_____

_____

_____

_____

_____

_____

_____

Day 15

Sit In Your Wound

How many would have failed except that hope sustained them through the darkness…until light could dawn.

~ Joan Walsh Anglund

Once you choose hope, anything is possible.

~ Christopher Reeve

You may be feeling vulnerable and shaken in the wake of your grief. Fear and vulnerability often prevent us from allowing ourselves to truly feel the depth of our pain. We are not sure we can tolerate it or that we will survive if we allow ourselves to touch our deepest wounds. It seems as if anesthetizing, minimizing, or ignoring the wound altogether is easier than to risk irritating it by touching it directly.

Yet it is necessary during this grief journey that you allow yourself to sit in your wound and touch the pain of grief gently, compassionately, and regularly. Sitting in your wound will open your heart, and open hearts naturally have hope. Hope will surface after you allow yourself to fully experience the woundedness that this loss has brought into your life.

Sitting in your wound is about being willing to encounter and embrace your deepest pain. Embracing the pain is an important part of healing in grief. Pain that is not embraced burrows deeper. Sometimes it festers and infiltrates your mood, your attitude, and your ability to relate to others with a compassionate heart. Sometimes the pain grows, and new pain is piled upon it. This pile-up of grief and pain can feel like a weight or burden that you carry around needlessly.

Yes, sitting in your wound means feeling the tightness in your chest, the emptiness in your heart, the deep sadness—not all at once and not for long lengths of time, so that the wound consumes you, but feeling and touching your wound in doses.

Hope smiles on the threshold of the year to come, whispering that it will be happier.

~ Alfred Lord Tennyson

Listen now to the gentle whispers of hope.

~ Charles D. Brodhead

It means dosing yourself with the pain, letting it surface, be felt, released momentarily, moving away from it for a while, and then allowing it to rise again.

Don't let fear stop you from sitting in your wound momentarily. Take the opportunity when it surfaces naturally to experience whatever is coming up for you, be it sadness, anger, hurt, helplessness, loneliness, confusion, or some other mix of emotions. Trust that it will soften. Make opportunities where you put yourself in places that invite the grief to surface— listening to a certain song, looking through a photo album, going to the cemetery, being in the space where the person you loved and lost used to spend time. Stop avoiding everything, everyone, and everyplace that brings the pain to the surface.

Yes, give yourself permission to sit in your wound and make room for hope. Allow the emotional pain to surface, freely expressed, little by little, until you find that you are carrying less, holding in less, and walking with a heart that is no longer consumed with grief. Let your heart be filled with hope instead.

Personal Reflection on Hope

What are the fears that arise when I think about allowing myself to sit in my wound? What are things I can do today that will help me sit in my wound, experience my grief in doses, and allow my heart to heal?

_____

_____

_____

_____

_____

_____

_____

_____

_____

_____

_____

_____

_____

_____

Day 16

Recognize You Are the Keeper of Your Life Force

When you're depressed, the whole body is depressed, and it translates to the cellular level. The first objective is to get your energy up, and you can do it through play. It's one of the most powerful ways of breaking up hopelessness and bringing energy into the situation.

~ O. Carl Simonton

Hope is patience with the lamp lit.

~ Tertullian

At your core is a source of energy that brings you to life. This life force or divine spark that you carry is what others feel from you when they are in your presence. Your divine spark radiates through your words, your actions, your thoughts, your mood, and your interactions. Your divine spark influences your entire way of being in the world.

Your divine spark belongs to you, and it is up to you to keep the flame lit and burning brightly. When we are suffering, as we do when loss enters our lives, our divine spark is naturally muted or, in some situations, extinguished, as in the shadow of grief. Those around us can see, hear, and feel this from us. You may have even felt your divine spark change when you were first confronting the reality that someone you love deeply had died.

The shadow of grief has muted, or perhaps completely extinguished, your zest for life, your love of life, your hope for the future. You may feel like you have less energy and feel irritable or a sense of sadness or emptiness. It is not always easy to spend time in the presence of others whose divine spark is muted; others may not be sure how to help you right now. But people love you, and they will continue to be with you despite this temporary state of being.

When we feel muted, turning our life over to others to take care of us seems easiest and sometimes feels necessary. Asking for help from supportive others is necessary at certain points

Hope works in these ways: it looks for the good in people instead of harping on the worst; it discovers what can be done instead of grumbling about what cannot; it regards problems, large or small, as opportunities; it pushes ahead when it would be easy to quit; it "lights the candle" instead of "cursing the darkness."

~ Anonymous

in our grief journey. But even as others help you get through the day-to-day tasks, ultimately you are the keeper of your own life force. Your divine spark, that which gives you expression, creativity, and momentum, is not something another can take care of or revive for you. Just as no other person can breathe for you, no other person can be the keeper of your life force.

Because you hold the key, there is hope for reviving it. No one can do it for you, and no one can keep you from it. Though you cannot change the way you feel, you can consciously remind yourself to pay attention to your life force, your muted divine spark. Listen to what it is teaching you and be aware of the energy you are radiating out into the world. When you do this, you will find that as the keeper of your life force, you must nurture your divine spark and love yourself through this very difficult time.

In the midst of winter I found there was, within me, an invincible summer.

~ Albert Camus

Personal Reflection on Hope

Describe how this loss has impacted your divine spark. What can you do to give attention to this core part of who you are right now?

_____

_____

_____

_____

_____

_____

_____

_____

_____

_____

_____

_____

_____

Day 17

Reignite Your Divine Spark

*Through the days ahead, my new sense of hope,
now nearly an extinguished spark, will grow brighter
and larger, and it will warm my life as it has the
lives of countless other survivors before me.*

~ Carol Staudacher

Yes, the shadow of grief has veiled your true essence or life force. The light your divine spark typically radiates in the world may be at an all-time low. Walking in the world with a muted, perhaps even extinguished, divine spark can feel discouraging and disheartening. It's as if the light inside of you has lost its power or the candle that lights your life path has been blown out. Others can feel it when they are with you. More importantly, you can feel the dimness and dreariness that ensues a muting of one's divine spark.

You don't have to live this way, walking around with a faint inner ember, for the rest of your life. In fact, an important part of your grief journey is actively reconnecting with life again, reinvesting in those aspects of living that brought love, happiness, and passion into your days and nights. You may have forgotten what it feels like when your divine spark is shining brightly. Give yourself the chance to feel this again, even if only for a moment.

As you find ways to actively engage in life again, your light will be rekindled and shine a little more brightly with each passing day. As you actively engage, even in small ways, you will generate a renewed sense of hope because you will feel the light inside of you again. Feeling even a little light will lead you to seek more and find what will help that fire burn brightly.

The light will burn brightly again as you work through your grief. Yes, right now you are bereaved. Bereaved literally means

Hope, like the gleaming taper's light, adorns and cheers our way; and still, as darker grows the night, emits a lighter ray.

~ Oliver Goldsmith

to feel "torn apart" and "to have special needs." As I've honored the stories of thousands of mourners and encountered loss in my own life, I have found that an important part of finding our inner light again involves giving attention to six central needs of mourning. As you meet these six central needs—acknowledge the reality of the death, embrace the pain of the loss, transform your relationship with the person who died to one of memory, develop a new self-identity, search for meaning around this loss, and seek ongoing support—you will be actively moving through grief toward life. (See my book *The Journey Through Grief* for a more in-depth exploration of these six central needs of mourning.) These needs are like steppingstones that allow you to light the wick of your divine spark as you walk through the wilderness of your grief.

To hope is to enjoy.

~ Jacques Delille

Personal Reflection on Hope

Am I working through the six central needs of mourning? Which need is the most difficult for me and whom can I seek support from as I continue to move through grief and toward reigniting my divine spark?

_____

_____

_____

_____

_____

_____

_____

_____

_____

_____

_____

_____

Day 18

Move From Head to Heart

Hope sees the invisible, feels the intangible,
and achieves the impossible.

~ Anonymous

When you are sorrowful, look again in your
heart, and you shall see that in truth you are
weeping for that which has been your delight.

~ Kahlil Gibran

When we experience loss, there is a natural desire to try to understand it. "How" and "why" questions are your head's way of trying to make sense out of all of this. The mind desperately seeks answers because answers provide an intellectual understanding. And an intellectual understanding of this situation might lessen some of the out-of-control feelings and helplessness that are naturally present.

You may have a desire to learn more about the grief process and how it typically unfolds for mourners. Naturally, your head wants to know, "How long does grief take?" and "What can I expect to feel as I move through the process?" If you feel the need to review the circumstances of the death over and over again in your head, don't let this surprise you. Your head wants to know what contributed to the death and what could have been done to change the outcome.

This death, this loss, is not something that your head will be able to understand completely. Your mind is trying to make sense of things that we are incapable of fully understanding on an intellectual level. Why? Because grief is not strictly an intellectual experience. Grief radiates through your entire being—heart, mind, body, soul, and spirit.

Your head is the part of you that is constantly in search of answers, seeking balance, order, and meaning. Understanding this loss in your head is very different from integrating it into your heart. Intellectual understanding of the death experience

We judge a man's wisdom by his hope.

~ Ralph Waldo Emerson

Hope is sweet-minded and sweet-eyed. It draws pictures; it weaves fancies; it fills the future with delight.

~ Henry Ward Beecher

does not always accompany integration in your heart and soul. Allowing your head to lead you through this grief journey will make the process challenging and frustrating.

Moving through grief means allowing your head to seek answers (because that is what it's designed to do) but knowing that those answers are not what will bring you to hope. Moving through grief means encouraging your heart to feel and being present to those aspects of your grief that are unanswerable. Remember, the word heart literally means "well of reception."

Remind yourself that mourning requires that, at times, you consciously shift from your head (from trying to "get it") to your heart (to trying to "feel it"). This shift allows you to make movement through grief rather than spin in intellectual circles. Movement will elicit hope that you will not dwell in the depths of your grief forever. Even when the movement you make is small or brief, you will feel the hope that progression is possible. You are creating the divine momentum needed to be transformed by this loss and discover renewed meaning and purpose in your life.

Personal Reflection on Hope

What is my understanding of how I may be managing my grief in my head versus experiencing my grief in my heart? If I discover that I am "in my head," what can I do to move to my heart?

Day 19

Look for Open Doors

With hope all things are possible.

~ The Holy Bible

I have seen what a laugh can do. It can transform almost unbearable tears into something bearable, even hopeful.

~ Anonymous

Some days it may feel as if you are all alone with your grief. Immediately after your loss, you may have experienced a surge of support from others. People welcome you to call them "if you need anything" and compassionately remind you that they are "here whenever you need." They are letting you know that the door is open to you and you will find support, help, love, hope, and reassurance on the other side. Naturally, as time goes by, the love and attention of others slows down, and eventually it may even feel as if it stops completely.

Though you may question if the door is still open to you because others are not coming around or calling as often, let me reassure you it probably is. The only way to find the answer is to reach out to family, friends, and support people whom you feel are out of touch.

It may also be time for you to look for new doors to open. Your life has been changed forever by this loss, and loss leads to transformation. Transformation literally means to experience an entire change in form. Transformation presents new doors. These doors may lead you to new places, new people, or new experiences that you didn't know were possible.

When we open doors, we can find new ways to re-engage in life and living. You may discover people you enjoy spending time with and make arrangements to be with them more. You could find a new interest or renew your interest in something you enjoyed long ago, such as playing tennis, painting, gardening,

We should not let our fears hold us
back from pursuing our hopes.

~ John F. Kennedy

Hope opens dark doors and companions
you into the light of a new day.

~ Alan D. Wolfelt

or volunteering. You might unearth a project that you want to complete but have not been able to for some reason. Behind a door you may be reminded of a place you want to visit but have not had the time or opportunity to explore because life was getting in the way.

Don't be afraid to look for doors and, more importantly, to open them when you are standing in front of them. Try this exercise to help you bring these opportunities into your life today:

Close your eyes and imagine yourself sitting in a room where there are doors on every wall. Though you have no idea what is beyond each door, each has something new for you to experience. Opening new doors can be frightening. Let your fear enter the room. Let it sit there with you as you contemplate which direction to go first. But don't let your fear prevent you from taking a chance, creating an opportunity for yourself by opening the doors. Choose one and open it… what do you see?

Personal Reflection on Hope

As I open new doors, what are the ways I am encouraging myself to reengage in life and living?

_____

_____

_____

_____

_____

_____

_____

_____

_____

_____

_____

_____

Day 20

Allow Yourself To Surrender

Love in all its forms is hope.

~ Amy Bloom

To surrender means to allow something to *be as it is*. It means sitting with what IS even when what you feel is painful, confusing, anxiety-provoking, sad, overwhelming, or unpleasant in some way. For some, surrender sounds counterintuitive, as if surrendering will hurt more than it will help by resulting in comfort and healing. Moving away from rather than surrendering to unpleasant experiences in life is commonly encouraged by those family and friends who aren't familiar with the value of surrendering.

But surrendering to the thoughts and feelings that surface in the face of loss helps you move through your grief. Surrendering will be uncomfortable at first, but as you continue to practice letting your emotions surface and allowing them to stay, it will become easier over time. In practicing surrender, start by asking yourself, "Am I willing to be uncomfortable?" and "Can I tolerate feeling unpleasant emotions, at least momentarily?"

You will know that you are surrendering to the pain of your grief in the moments that you consciously move toward it rather than away from it. You will no longer feel the knee-jerk reaction to hide, fix, anesthetize, or move away from it. When your emotions surface, you will allow yourself to experience them.

At this difficult time, there are many things you can surrender to. Your emotional pain. Your broken heart. Your confused mind. Your questioning spirit. When you surrender, you invite

Keep your face to the sunshine and you cannot see the shadow. It's what sunflowers do.

~ Helen Keller

hope into your life because you are not working so hard to keep things at bay. When you try to keep your underlying feelings distant from your inner self, you are unable to touch the hope that resides in your heart.

Allow yourself to experience the pain, to feel the brokenness of your heart, to attend to the thoughts that swirl around in your mind and the questions that come from your soul. When you are able to allow yourself to do this in doses, your grief is tolerable. Each day, spend a few moments surrendering to the parts of your grief that are most difficult—feeling them, experiencing them, and just simply being with them.

Personal Reflection on Hope

Write below about your willingness or lack of willingness to be uncomfortable, to surrender to your painful feelings of grief.

_____

_____

_____

_____

_____

_____

_____

_____

_____

_____

_____

_____

_____

_____

Day 21

Carry the Light Of Hope

*To keep a lamp burning, we have
to keep putting oil in it.*

~ Mother Teresa

*Hope begins in the dark, the stubborn hope that if you
just show up and try to do the right thing, the dawn will
come. You wait and watch and work: you don't give up.*

~ Anne Lamott

The journey through grief is not as orderly and predictable as others sometimes tell us. The "stages" of grief that are so often talked about are actually not intended to guide mourners on a straight path to healing. You are likely to experience some of the emotions described in the stages of grief model—such as despair, anger, and denial—but overall your grief will not be as orderly and predictable as the stages model would suggest.

Grief is more often like a walk through the wilderness. It can be dark and uncertain. You may even feel frightened, and the journey can be daunting at times. As you enter the wilderness of your grief, you will have a hard time seeing what is up ahead, and you will find yourself meandering rather than walking a straight line through the stages of grief. Some days, putting one foot in front of the other may be all you are able to do. And that's okay. In fact, it's a normal part of walking through the wilderness of grief.

You will need something to help you shed some light along the way, and that light is hope. When you carry hope with you in the wilderness, you can see farther ahead. You may not see your final destination, but hope can light the path enough to allow you to see that there is a way out. The way out is through—through the darkness and into the light.

The depth of your sorrow is symptomatic of a healthy soul, not a disturbed soul. Deep sorrow keeps you more aware of the preciousness of the present moment and clarifies what

When it is dark enough, you can see the stars.

~ Charles A. Beard

Hope is eternal. All the darkness of the world cannot put out the light of one small candle.

~ Unknown

is truly important in your life. Slowing down opens you to experience the wonders that surround you. Allow life in the present moment to be a gift of grace to you.

When you allow yourself to look into the future and to identify aspects of the future that will bring love, light, and happiness into your heart again, you are igniting hope and carrying it with you. Take a moment to consider the things, the people, the events, and the experiences that will light your path tomorrow and the next day, and each day after that. Are you planning to meet a friend for coffee or dinner? Is there a celebration that you will be a part of? Are there any trips planned with friends or family in the near future? Is there a benefit in honor of the person who died that will surround you with compassionate support? What are you looking forward to? If the answer is *nothing*, ask yourself what you can plan that you will look forward to.

There are countless opportunities, big and small, to experience something that will bring light into your life as you walk through the wilderness of your grief. Plan something that will bring a spark into your life and let that light of hope guide you on your next step of this journey.

Personal Reflection on Hope

What are a few of the rays of light in my near or distant future? If there are none, what can I bring into my life that will feel like a ray of light, like something to look forward to?

_____

_____

_____

_____

_____

_____

_____

_____

_____

_____

_____

_____

Day 22

Seek Solitude

When I feel battered by overwhelming grief, I can restore myself through solitude, quietness, and peace. Alone time allows my body, mind, and heart to be rejuvenated. The privacy of the moment allows me to discover the reason to live again.

~ Alan D. Wolfelt

Solitude is not something you must hope for in the future. Rather, it is a deepening of the present, and unless you look for it in the present, you will never find it.

~ Thomas Merton

You may have mixed feeling about being alone right now. At times, being away from crowds, noise, or the demands of others may bring you relief. Other times, when no one else is sharing a certain moment with you—but you wish someone was, loneliness may start setting in.

But being alone (and feeling alone) is very different than being in solitude. Being in solitude means the focus in the moment is on YOU. It does not feel as if you are alone or others have deserted you in this moment, because there is no desire to have another join you. There is no recognition that you are without others, because being with yourself is enough. In solitude, all you need is you and the quietness that surrounds you. Solitude is an opportunity to embrace a moment, an experience, a place unaccompanied by anyone other than yourself.

When others are in the space that surrounds you, no matter how supportive and loving they are, it is difficult to embrace yourself. The presence of others can distract you, demand things of you, and pull you away from yourself. In fact, this is why some mourners *avoid* solitude. They seek the distraction of constantly being in the presence of others in an effort, conscious or unconscious, to avoid the grief that naturally bubbles up when they are alone.

In solitude, the only needs that are in that space are yours. The only distractions are those that exist within you—your thoughts and physical sensations. The only sounds are what your voice, your body, and your mind are whispering. And it is important to create the time and space to acknowledge and listen to these essential whispers.

Seeking solitude gives you the opportunity to truly experience you, your sense of *self*. There is a sense of peace that can come into your heart and soul when you give yourself permission to spend time with your self.

Throughout your grief journey, you will have periods when you feel you are completely on your own with this, you alone have to navigate the way through an unpleasant surge of emotion, a painful memory, or an event that triggers thoughts about the person who died. As C.S. Lewis reflected in his classic book *A Grief Observed*, "My heart and body are crying out, come back, come back." Nurturing yourself with solitude can make it easier to get through these periods. Solitude brings you hope because as you experience it, you will know that you can make it through no matter what. You will make it through no matter who is or is not there for you. Even when others are absent, you will make it through because you know it's possible to offer comfort and support to yourself.

Please understand that there is a difference between solitude and isolation. Seeking intermittent solitude is part of a healthy response to inner turmoil. Self-imposed isolation, on the other hand, is a sign of depression. The difference is in the length and breadth of the alone time. If you find yourself unable to interact with others for weeks at a time or sustain loving relationships, you may be experiencing deep depression and should seek professional help.

Take a moment to make a list of the places you can go to experience true solitude and spend a few minutes being in one of these places at least once each day, reflecting on the gift of solitude. Here are a few you might consider.

- *At a park, under a tree*
- *In your car*
- *In your church, synagogue, or temple when there is no service*
- *Walking around the cemetery*
- *Sitting on your deck or porch*
- *Taking a hot bath or shower*
- *Watching the sunrise*
- *On a bike ride*
- *In any room in your home, when no one else is present*

Everything that is done in the world is done by hope.

~ Martin Luther

Personal Reflection on Hope

Go to a place that allows you to bask in solitude. Now, ask yourself what comes up for you. What is it like in the core of your being?

_____

_____

_____

_____

_____

_____

_____

_____

_____

_____

_____

_____

Day 23

Practice Gratitude

Practice hope. As hopefulness becomes a habit,
you can achieve a permanently happy spirit.

~ Norman Vincent Peale

Hope is not the conviction that something will
turn out well, but the certainty that something
makes sense regardless of how it turns out.

~ Václav Havel

After experiencing a devastating loss, it is natural to wonder, "What could I possibly have to be grateful for right now?" After all, gratitude is something you feel when things are going well, and your time of grief is not such a time. Gratitude is what is expressed when you appreciate what is happening in your life, and appreciation is not likely something you feel in the aftermath of this loss.

Though it seems implausible to feel gratitude at the same time as grief, gratitude is present. Even though your world has been torn apart, you are surrounded by people and things that you have gratitude for. Identifying and acknowledging what we appreciate right now is more important than ever.

Take a moment to look around and discover where you can practice gratitude.

Look at your relationships. Who is someone you appreciate having in your life right now?

Look around your home. What is something you own that you are thankful that you have in your life because it offers you comfort?

Look at the actions of others. What has someone done for you, to offer encouragement or love that you appreciate?

Look at yourself. What quality in yourself is shining through and helping you through this difficult time?

Look at the ordinary things in your life. What makes your life easier on a daily basis?

Your hopes, dreams, and aspirations are legitimate. They are trying to take you airborne, above the clouds, above the storms, if you only let them.

~ William James

If these questions do not help you discover what you are grateful for despite your grief, simply try another approach. Gratitude can grow when you practice extending it in situations you might not normally be grateful for. Practice expressing in your mind or out loud what is so ordinary that gratitude doesn't even cross your mind when you encounter it.

- A Certain Person in Your Life. Write a thank you card to someone you love just because he or she is in your life. Don't wait until he's done something for you or given you something.

- Nature. Take a hike and be thankful for the trail; watch the sunrise and be thankful you can see the vibrant colors.

- Your Body and Mind. Thank your body for functioning even when it feels exhausted. Thank your mind for helping you filter and take in only the information you need right now.

- Children. Thank a child for something simple like sharing her laugh or smile, for giving you a high-five or a hug, or for reminding you how important it is to play.

- The Person Who Died. Write a letter or say a prayer of gratitude to the person who died, thanking him for what he brought to your life.

- God's Love for You. The greatest love of all for many of us in God's love. Acknowledge God's love for you and how even in the darkest of times God is still there. In hope, you can trust His promise, "I will never leave you or forsake you."

You can have gratitude even in the shadow of your grief. Practicing gratitude elicits hope. No matter what life brings, life is filled with things to appreciate.

Personal Reflection on Hope

Use the space below to openly acknowledge what you have gratitude for in your life. Consider starting a daily gratitude journal to allow you to appreciate what you do have in your life despite your grief and loss.

_____

_____

_____

_____

_____

_____

_____

_____

_____

_____

Day 24

Listen to and Feel Hope

The very least you can do in your life is to figure out what you hope for. And the most you can do is live inside that hope. Not admire it from a distance but live right in it, under its roof.

~ Barbara Kingsolver

Yes, hope is something you can actually hear...if you listen. When you practice consciously listening to what is going on around you, will be amazed at how much hope is being spread in the air. You will hear it in music, writing, and conversations going on around you.

Listen for hope in conversation with friends and colleagues. Find hope in a favorite poem, song lyrics, or a children's story you read as a child. Hear hope in the movies you watch with friends, kids, or family members. Listen for hope in the conversations being held in coffee houses or between a parent and a child.

Listen to the rhythm, not just the words in music that moves you; you will find hope there too. Hear hope in nature—in the wind, the birds, the sound of a waterfall. Hope can be heard in the laughter of the kids playing on the playground or at the pool.

Anywhere you are, hope is there and can be heard if you stop, close your eyes, and focus on listening for it. Wherever you are, take a moment to close your eyes and listen. Is may be easier to hear hope with your eyes closed so that you are not distracted by your other senses. It may simply be that you hear your own voice whispering words of hope to you.

Don't be afraid to seek out experiences, people, or places where you know hope is being shared.

Perhaps they are not stars, but rather openings in heaven where the love of our lost ones pours through and shines upon us to let us know they are happy.

— Eskimo Proverb

- *Call a friend and ask him to tell you something hopeful.*

- *Download a song that sings of hope…make a hope playlist or make a hopeful song the ringtone on your cell phone.*

- *Find a book of poetry on hope and read the poems out loud with your friends or family members.*

Bring hope into your life through your ears. When hope comes to you through this sense, it resonates on a different level than when you see it or touch it.

You can also feel hope. I am reminded of the story of the young man who is flying a kite.

> The wind was brisk and large clouds filled the sky. The kite ascended high above the clouds until it could no longer be seen. Someone inquired of the young man, "What are you doing?" He responded without hesitation, "I am flying a kite."
>
> "But how can you be sure? You cannot see the kite," the bystander noted.
>
> "No," said the young man. "I cannot see it, but every so often I feel a tug on my hands. So you see, I know it is there high up in the sky."

Yes, sometimes you can't see hope, but you feel it is there!

Personal Reflection on Hope

As you listen for hope, what do you discover? As you feel hope, what do you discover?

_____

_____

_____

_____

_____

_____

_____

_____

_____

_____

_____

_____

_____

Day 25

Touch the Hand of Hope

Hope is faith holding out its hand in the dark.

~ George Iles

*Hope is the companion of power, and
mother of success; for who so hopes strongly
has within him the gift of miracles.*

~ Samuel Smiles

If only hope were human in form and had a hand that could actually be touched. Inviting hope into our lives and living with it would be much easier if it were concrete, more tangible in nature. Though hope does not have a hand that we can reach out and touch, you can find it in the hands of those who are present to you during this difficult time.

Hope is there, in the hands of a child.
Hold a child's hand.

In the hands of your clergyperson, hope exists. Hold hands as he or she gives you support.

Hope sits in your own hands.
Hold your hands in prayer.

You will find hope in the hands of a supportive friend. Hold hands as you share the story of your loss.

Neighbors and friends possess hands filled with hope. Take a moment to shake hands, wave, or hug someone and allow hope to be passed on to you through the touch of another.

Your precious pets offer paws of love. Welcome their affection and embrace the comfort and hope they offer.

Find those hands that are filled with hope. Touch them and allow them to reach out to you so that hope can be passed on to you. Remember, hands everywhere hold hope for you. Reach out and it will be yours to take in.

Personal Reflection on Hope

Who in my circle of friends and family has touched me in ways that allow me to feel safe and supported at this time in my life? What has that been like for me?

Hope means letting people in—allowing myself to touch and be touched. Then people can offer me hope, inner strength, and the gift of love.

~ Alan D. Wolfelt

Day 26

Embrace Transformation

Hope has engendered a life to start again.

~ Nancy Fusillo

*The natural flights of the human mind are not
from pleasure to pleasure but from hope to hope.*

~ Samuel Johnson

We are transformed by the losses in our lives. When the person you love died, your life changed in many ways. Daily routines changed. Relationships changed. Interactions within your family changed. You changed. The way you feel about life and about death may be changing. Your beliefs about God, life after death, and the purpose of living may even be in the process of changing. Some of the changes you are experiencing may also be bringing about what are called "secondary losses." Loss of a sense that the world is a safe place, loss of financial security, and loss of identity as a parent, partner, and sibling are among the secondary losses that many mourners encounter.

Experiencing so many losses in a brief period of time can be overwhelming. The transformations in your life can leave you feeling incredibly powerless and out of control. You are not in control of the "how," the "when," or the "why" related to all of the changes occurring within and around you. You may want the changes to stop; you are on change overload. You are faced with the need to change so many aspects of your daily life, integrating new ways of being with the old.

When change is occurring in our lives, we can begin to feel empowered and hopeful again when we are able to embrace the transformations that are unfolding. They are happening; they are in motion. The more you resist changes that naturally come when someone you love dies, the more exhausting, frustrating, and intense the grief journey.

The Grand essentials of happiness are: something to do, something to love, and something to hope for.

~ Allan K. Chalmers

Each day comes bearing its own gifts. Untie the ribbons.

~ Ruth Ann Schabacker

You will know that you are embracing transformation when you observe yourself:

- acknowledging to yourself that change is a natural part of grief.

- identifying the various changes that are present in your life, though they are changes you didn't ask for and wouldn't have invited if you would have had the choice.

- opening to all of the emotions, even the most unpleasant ones.

- talking about how this loss is impacting your home life, your work life, you relationships, and your own personal growth.

- feeling hope that the changes you've experienced and that are in the process of unfolding will lead you to a more peaceful place than where you were early in your grief.

You are undergoing a complete change in form. Through this process, loss brings the promise of something new for you. Give yourself permission to wrap your arms and heart around the transformations, even those that are most difficult to accept.

Invite yourself to improve yourself along the journey. Strive to become better regardless of what challenges you face. Be grateful for and embrace your unique life gifts. Grow in the very depth of your soul, in your ways of showing compassion to others who have come to know loss, and in your capacity to discover renewed joy. Redirect your life story so that as you live life with a courageous spirit, you continue to grow and change.

Personal Reflection on Hope

How have I been transformed by this death? What have I done
to embrace this transformation?

_____

_____

_____

_____

_____

_____

_____

_____

_____

_____

*This death has made me look at what is important
in life. How very important are the choices I make
each moment both to myself and to those I love.*

~ Alan D. Wolfelt

Day 27

Celebrate Life

May we celebrate each new day and the hope it brings.

~ Brenda Wiseman & June Morse

Things never go so well that one should have no fear,
and never so ill that one should have no hope.

~ Turkish Proverb

It is difficult to describe the hurt you feel knowing that the person who died is no longer physically part of your life. When someone you love dies, you realize how precious life and love truly are. You've been reminded that life always eventually comes to an end.

Loss reminds us that the only time we are guaranteed is right now. Now is the opportunity to celebrate what you have. Now is the time to celebrate life—your life and the life you share with the person who died. Every day is an opportunity to celebrate. Celebrating life is one way of honoring that person's memory and inviting hope into your world—hope that although that person's physical life has ended, his or her memory will go on, and the love he or she brought into the world will be celebrated by those whose lives were touched.

Celebrating means doing something to commemorate, observe, and acknowledge life. Celebration is something that you can do with or without others. If you don't feel that being around a large group of people right now would be helpful, it's okay to find ways to celebrate with a small group, a single friend, or in the presence of no one other than yourself. Celebrations can be large or they can be small. You can celebrate for a moment or for days. How and with whom you choose to celebrate is entirely up to you.

The human body experiences a powerful
gravitational pull in the direction of hope.

~ Norman Cousins

Hope is a happiness held in the heart
When happiness seems to be gone.
Hope is a quiet joy deep within encouraging us to go on.

~ Anonymous

There are many simple ways that you can celebrate life today. You might find yourself celebrating life by:

- *Going on a hike and breathing in the fresh air. As you breathe you can say out loud to yourself and the world, "It's great to be alive!"*

- *Helping someone who has a difficult time getting around on his or her own. As you help, celebrate the fact that we all have obstacles in our lives, but they do not have to prevent us from participating in life fully.*

- *Celebrating the ordinary things about your day—a cup of coffee, sitting by a fire, being in the presence of a comforting friend, watching the sunset, talking a walk, or lighting a candle.*

As you take time to celebrate being alive, you may find yourself thinking about the person who died. You might long to have this person there with you physically and feel deep sadness around the reality that he or she is not physically present for this celebration. Invite your memories of the person who died in. Allow them to be a part of your celebration. Let yourself experience the pangs of grief and consider what this person taught you about life and living. Embracing your memories will help you transform the physical relationship you once shared with the person who died into one of loving, gentle memory.

Personal Reflection on Hope

Life is worth celebrating. How can I celebrate being alive? What has this death taught me about the importance of life, living, and loving?

Day 28

Be Open to Possibilities

Hope arouses as nothing else can arouse
a passion for the possible.

~ Anonymous

When you open yourself to possibilities, you open yourself to hope. Hope is about believing in possibilities, knowing you have choices, and seeing more than one option when you are looking into the future. Hope is about knowing there is potential for something more.

Take a moment to ask yourself,

"What is possible right now in my life?"

"What choices am I facing?"

"In deciding on the next steps in my life path, what options do I have to choose from?"

Exploring what is possible can open a floodgate of information, allowing hope to float in. Here are some ways to practice opening to possibilities:

- Ask specific questions about the loss that will help you see what is possible beyond what you are feeling in the present moment. Questions like: Is it possible that one day my pain will not feel so deep and raw? YES! Is it possible that one day I will make it through a day without tears? YES! Is it possible that one day I will be able to talk about the person who died without feeling so sad? YES! Is it possible that one day it will be easy to get out of bed again and face the day? YES! Is it possible that one day I will be able to sleep through the night? YES! Is it possible that one day I will not carry around this much anger

True hope dwells on the possible, even when life seems to be a plot written by someone who wants to see how much adversity we can overcome.

~ Anonymous

inside? YES! Is it possible that one day I will be able to help someone else who feels torn apart by grief? YES! Stay open to these possibilities.

- Look to see what others have done before you. If it's been done, it's possible. Do you know others who have experienced a similar loss and have found ways to integrate it into their life? Do you know anyone who has felt lost in her grief and found her way out? Talk with others who have journeyed through grief about how their experience felt in the beginning compared to how it feels now in their life.

- Look back to see what you have done that at some point you thought you could not do. You did it. It was possible. Consider things that you never thought you would accomplish in your life but you did. What did it take to do this? How did you make what seemed impossible possible?

Our imagination is the only limit to what we can hope to have in the future.

~ Charles F. Kettering

Personal Reflection on Hope

Write below what is possible in your life right now. Ask yourself:
Even in the face of adversity and grief, what is possible?

_____

_____

_____

_____

_____

_____

_____

_____

_____

_____

_____

_____

_____

Day 29

Spread Your Wings

Hope spreads her wings in unfathomable seas.

~ Unknown

This loss may feel heavy and burdensome at times. That feeling of being grounded from flight or brought to your knees by this experience will not be a constant in this grief journey. It will lessen as you allow yourself to embrace your pain and authentically mourn. You will find relief from this feeling of being grounded in moments when you open your wings and spread them enough to take brief flights into a space that is new to you.

Taking flight into the unknown might sound like the last thing you need right now. After all, the mysteries of grief (what is unknown, unfamiliar, and unanswered) are often the most difficult parts of grief to cope with. Sitting in complete darkness or "liminal space" (that place betwixt and between) for long periods of time can be unbearable. We can only deal with what we know, so any answer, even if it's incomplete, can bring relief as we move through our grief.

Even if the unknown frightens you, don't let fear keep you from experiencing relief. When you are going through a difficult time and feeling weighed down, allowing yourself to experience something new can be refreshing. It can lighten your heart, your mind, and your soul from the weight of grief momentarily.

Spreading your wings means flying toward something new. Moving toward something novel can ignite hope because it allows you to see that you are still capable of flying. It allows

*There is nothing that fear and hope
do not permit men to do.*

~ Marquis De Vauvenargues

*Hope is a light that burns in the night
in a place where a miracle starts,
And every good thing will come in its time...
As long as there's hope in our hearts.*

~ Anonymous

you to demonstrate to yourself that you are open to seeing what is out there. It reminds you that you are still alive and that there is more for you to see, more for you to do, more for you to experience. More is out there waiting for you. Here are some questions to get yourself thinking:

- *Can you think of a new group or club to get involved with?*
- *Is there something that you've always wanted to try but haven't?*
- *Is there an activity or hobby that you could try, even once?*
- *Are you interested in developing a new practice that you can put into use every day, such as meditation or yoga?*
- *What is something new that you could do each month to take care of yourself that you are not doing now (getting a monthly massage, drinking more water, working with a personal trainer)?*
- *Is there a place you could travel to that you have never been before?*

Make a list of ideas that would help you spread your wings. Circle the least frightening ones and do those first. You may not get to choose much about this grief process, but here you can have the freedom to choose. Choose the flights. Choose the order in which you take them. Choose whom to invite along for the ride or if you will do them alone.

Whatever you choose, the sheer fact that it is new to you will instill a sense of hope that you are alive, you are well, and you are willing to pave new paths for yourself. Bring hope by bringing something new into your life today!

Personal Reflection on Hope

How can I take flight by trying something new? Name something new you will try and when you will do it. Keep saying to yourself, "I can and will spread my wings."

_____

_____

_____

_____

_____

_____

_____

_____

_____

_____

_____

_____

_____

_____

Day 30

Rediscover Happiness

Three grand essentials to happiness in this life are something to do, something to love, and something to hope for.

~ Joseph Addison

Hope is a guide when we seem to be lost,
That can help us find our way.
Hope is a strong, immovable force
That our doubts and our fears cannot sway.

~ Anonymous

Happiness is not something that you can search for and find in the external world. It doesn't exist in any possession you own. It doesn't live in any particular achievement you've reached. It isn't sitting in the wealth you may have built. It cannot be handed to you by any person in your life. Happiness is something that exists *within you*. Only you have the capacity to feel it and nurture it toward its full potential.

Happiness is what brings us joy. When someone we love dies, it can feel as if the loss drains every ounce of happiness right out of us. Loss leaves us feeling empty, weary, and depleted. Yet, even when it feels as if the happiness is gone, you can be assured it is still there. Grief does not consume happiness. But it does cast a dark cloud over us, making that happiness we felt before a little harder to find.

My home is on a mountaintop in the Rocky Mountains of Colorado, a little over 5,000 feet high. There have been many times when I have seen clouds over the plains just below me. Some mornings I wake up to discover that I am in the sunshine, but the plains below me are covered with clouds. At times, I even witness thunderstorms down below while I enjoy the lovely sunshine as I sit on my deck. Yes, sometimes the clouds of grief and loss temporarily block you from experiencing happiness. In some ways, I think the clouds symbolize the spiritual forces that reflect the muting of your divine spark. But underneath the veil of the clouds, happiness is there, just waiting to be rediscovered.

In the night of death, hope sees a star, and listening love can hear the rustle of a wing.

~ Robert Ingersoll

Sometimes I wonder: Does laughter have a place in my healing? Laughter cleanses my soul and mends my heart. It connects me to the world around me. When I allow myself levity, I discover I am alive.

~ Alan D. Wolfelt

As you rediscover the sources of happiness that live within you, hope will not be far behind. Happiness is a friend of hope, and often the two are inseparable. Rediscovering happiness in big and small ways will uplift and energize you. It will allow you to live with expression and animation as you walk through the world. When you carry happiness, it shows!

When you have happy energy, it draws others in. On the contrary, when you feel sadness and gloom, it holds people at arm's length. And although no one can make someone else happy, when you bump into someone who or something that radiates happiness, it can help you reconnect with the happiness that is lying under the clouds of your grief.

The next time you observe someone enjoying an activity, remind yourself that you just bumped into happiness. Reflect on what activities once brought you joy and if these are something you can do right now. The next time you see someone laughing or being playful, stop and notice that you are bumping into happiness. Reflect on and remember some of the things that once brought laughter and play into your life. Consider making a plan to do one of these things again soon.

Yes, bump into happiness and reconnect with the happiness that resides within you. Your heart and soul will be glad you did!

Personal Reflection on Hope

Even as you experience the dark clouds of grief, look around
and ask yourself: What makes me happy? Find a trusted friend
to express some happiness to today. This will allow you to take
it from the inside to the outside.

_____

_____

_____

_____

_____

_____

_____

_____

_____

_____

_____

Closing Thoughts

Embrace an Attitude of Hope as
You Continue Your Journey

Look forward. Continue to grow. As long as you live, you have a future.

~ Boyd

Everything can be taken away from a man but one thing that lasts of human freedoms —to choose one's attitude in any given set of circumstances, to choose one's own way.

~ Victor Frankl

Your attitude about life, about death, and about your ability to cope with this profound loss has a tremendous impact on how this journey will feel for you. The attitude you carry and your physical, emotional, and spiritual experience of grief are so intertwined. In fact, they influence one another continuously. When there is a change in one, it often results in a change in the other.

Someone you love died, and the emotions of grief are continuously influencing your attitude toward life and living. This loss will likely lead to a number of changes in your attitudes about many things—yourself, your relationships, love, life after death, and God, among others. As your attitudes change, a change in your experiences will follow.

We are emotional beings, so we all experience emotion, even if that emotion isn't outwardly displayed. The way you feel and express emotions such as sadness, loneliness, helplessness, frustration, and fear most likely differ from the way a friend or someone else in your family experiences them. In part, this is because your attitudes guide what you think, believe, expect, and decide to respond to when emotion surfaces. Attitude also determines whether or not you sit in judgment of your own emotions and ways of expressing those feelings.

The attitude you carry is key to helping you find hope during your unfolding journey through grief. Attitude is what will guide the way you experience and cope with the emotional pain of this loss. Your attitude will also guide the way you interact with and accept support from others during this difficult time.

*The day the Lord created hope was probably
the same day he created Spring.*

~ Bern Williams

When you live with an attitude that says, "This is hopeless," you will find yourself focusing primarily on what is negative about your feelings, about others, about your situation, and about the world. If your attitude is anchored in a hopeless outlook, your thoughts are filled with fear and worry. Without doubt, this will take a toll on your body, mind, and spirit.

An optimistic or hope-filled outlook, on the other hand, will allow you to see the glimmers of goodness in each day, in the waves of emotions that ebb and flow, in each interaction you have with another, and generally in the world around you. Cultivating this hope-filled approach to your journey is a vital part of renewing your spirit and creating a life of meaning and purpose. A hopeful attitude as you continue to mourn can open many doors for you and help you enjoy each day of your life.

When you live with an attitude of hope, you will feel remarkably different than if you allow yourself to walk through life with an attitude of despair. When you are sad and your attitude is hopeful, you are certain your sadness will soften eventually. In contrast, a despairing attitude makes it so that you become preoccupied with your sadness and convince yourself that your sadness will always feel this overwhelming. When you are lonely yet carry the conviction of hope, you are aware that loneliness is a natural feeling when someone you love deeply is no longer present in your life. When you are confused, your attitude of hope will bring the expectation that answers will come as long as you keep asking the questions.

Yes, attitude is key to transforming your experience with grief. Change the way you perceive this experience of grief as you befriend an attitude of hope. You can get started on this path with a few simple steps:

- Become more aware of your attitudes toward grief. At the beginning or end of today, take a few minutes to finish the following sentences:

> *I think that my grief is…*
> *When I think about loss and grief, I believe that …*
> *I expect that my grief will be …*

- Take a moment to reflect on what you wrote and consider how these thoughts, beliefs, and expectations of grief are influencing you and how you feel on a day-to-day basis about living with grief.

- Consider how your emotions and feelings would be influenced if you were living with an attitude of hope.

- Describe at least one way in which you can practice living with an attitude of hope today!

Be Inspired by Hope

Hope creates inspiration to live your life with new possibilities. Each day can be embraced with meaning as you discover what inspires you to keep going even when confronted with grief and suffering. Hope embraced by inspiration eventually overcomes any fears that reside within you. And, when you are inspired in the depths of your being, you naturally ask yourself, "What is the purpose of my life?" Your soul's response can help you befriend this question and give you reason to go on living in a grace-filled state.

You can look for purpose in many places, but in my experience, it is often found when you share your unique, loving ways of being in the world with the people around you, both near and far. Bring your inspiration for life with you everywhere you go, and your hope will be contagious!

Explore the following signs and symptoms to see if you are befriending and being inspired by hope:

- You have the capacity to enjoy precious moments that touch your heart.
- You feel a sense of belonging in the world around you, as if the universe were embracing you.
- You experience a full range of emotions, from sadness to protest and anxiety to love and joy.
- You experience times when you are in contact with your inner sense of wisdom, love, and healing.
- You feel mysteriously supported and loved at times when you need it, keeping you open to the divine.
- You persevere even in the face of adversity. You create goals for yourself and set about accomplishing them with continued, patient effort.

- You experience a gentleness of spirit and kindness of heart. Kindness becomes a natural virtue you express in the world. Kindness adds hope-filled texture to every aspect of your life.

- You experience the beauty around you. You come to realize that this moment, this day, this relationship, and this life are all unique, exquisite, and unrepeatable. You can now embrace every moment.

- You are aware that your emotional and spiritual healing has transformed you and resulted in new energy in your body, nourishment in your mind, and illumination in your soul.

- You experience the unleashing of your inner power and divine spark. You radiate positive energy and engage in life in ways that connect you to the greater world of humanity. You feel alive, vibrant, and vital. While you have been wounded by your grief, you are still able to live with meaning and purpose in your life. Yes, with hope you can live an abundant life as your divine spark shines anew.

- You feel your heart opening up more each and every day. When your heart is open, you are receptive to what life brings you, both happy and sad. By "staying open," you create a gateway to your healing. You are able to celebrate the rays of a new light and a new beginning!

It can be easy to forget that hope is already within us. Perhaps we are well-served to remember to quiet ourselves and listen for that still, small voice of hope. Even though it can be naturally frightening, the most illuminating places we can go are within ourselves. So listen to yourself and listen to God and experience the magic of what you discover.

When you stop resisting, the challenges you face become your greatest teachers, and God becomes your greatest comfort. May this be so for you. Again, I hope we meet one day!

While grief never fully comes to an end, an attitude of hope helps me embrace my transformation and live my life from a place of hope, of meaning, and of purpose.

~ Alan D. Wolfelt

Personal Reflection on Hope

How can I commit myself to befriending an attitude of hope as my grief journey continues to unfold?

_____

_____

_____

_____

_____

_____

_____

_____

_____

_____

While grief never fully comes to an end, an attitude of hope helps me embrace my transformation and live my life from a place of hope, of meaning, and of purpose.

~ Alan D. Wolfelt

Start a Hope-Filled Support Group!

This book makes an ideal 12-week grief support group text. Have a get-started session, then meet once a week for 10 weeks and discuss three of the reflections each meeting. Hold a final meeting based on the Closing Thoughts section.

ALSO BY ALAN WOLFELT

The Journey Through Grief:
Reflections On Healing
SECOND EDITION

This revised, second edition of *The Journey Through Grief* takes Dr. Wolfelt's popular book of reflections and adds space for guided journaling, asking readers thoughtful questions about their unique mourning needs and providing room to write responses.

The Journey Through Grief is organized around the six needs that all mourners must yield to—indeed embrace—if they are to go on to find continued meaning in life and living. Following a short explanation of each mourning need is a series of brief, spiritual passages that, when read slowly and reflectively, help mourners work through their unique thoughts and feelings.

"The reflections in this book encourage you to think, yes, but to think with your heart and soul," writes Dr. Wolfelt. "They invite you to go to that spiritual place inside you and, transcending our mourning-avoiding society and even your own personal inhibitions about grief, enter deeply into the journey."

ISBN 978-1-879651-11-1 • hardcover • 176 pages • $21.95
(plus additional shipping and handling)

Companion
P R E S S

All Dr. Wolfelt's publications can be ordered by mail from:
Companion Press
3735 Broken Bow Road • Fort Collins, CO 80526
(970) 226-6050 • Fax 1-800-922-6051
www.centerforloss.com

Also by Alan Wolfelt

Healing Your Grieving Soul

100 Spiritual Practices for Mourners

Grief is in large part a spiritual struggle, and turning to spiritual practices in the face of loss helps many people find hope and healing. Following a helpful introduction about the role of spirituality in grief, this practical guide offers tips and activities on meditation, prayer, yoga, solitude and many more. Mourners who are feeling anxious might try breathing exercises. Those experiencing fatigue might try massage. Each idea is accompanied by a "carpe diem," which is a specific activity that the reader can try right that very moment to engage with her grief on the path to healing.

ISBN 978-1-879651-57-9 • 128 pages • softcover • $11.95

Companion
PRESS

All Dr. Wolfelt's publications can be ordered by mail from:
Companion Press
3735 Broken Bow Road • Fort Collins, CO 80526
(970) 226-6050 • Fax 1-800-922-6051
www.centerforloss.com

The Wilderness of Grief

Finding Your Way

A beautiful, hardcover gift book version of *Understanding Your Grief*

Understanding Your Grief provides a comprehensive exploration of grief and the ten essential touchstones for finding hope and healing your heart. *The Wilderness of Grief* is an excerpted version of *Understanding Your Grief*, making it approachable and appropriate for all mourners.

This concise book makes an excellent gift for anyone in mourning. On the book's inside front cover is room for writing an inscription to your grieving friend.

While some readers will appreciate the more in-depth *Understanding Your Grief*, others may feel overwhelmed by the amount of information it contains. For these readers we recommend *The Wilderness of Grief*. (Fans of *Understanding Your Grief* will also want a copy of *The Wilderness of Grief* to turn to in spare moments.)

The Wilderness of Grief is an ideal book for the bedside or coffee table. Pick it up before bed and read just a few pages. You'll be carried off to sleep by its gentle, affirming messages of hope and healing.

ISBN 978-1-879651-52-4 • 128 pages • hardcover • $15.95

Companion
PRESS

All Dr. Wolfelt's publications can be ordered by mail from:
Companion Press
3735 Broken Bow Road • Fort Collins, CO 80526
(970) 226-6050 • Fax 1-800-922-6051
www.centerforloss.com

Also by Alan Wolfelt

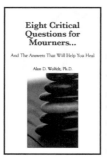

Eight Critical Questions for Mourners...
And the Answers That Will Help You Heal

When loss enters your life, you are faced with many choices. The questions you ask and the choices you make will determine whether you become among the "living dead" or go on to live until you die. If you are going to integrate grief into your life, it helps to recognize what questions to ask yourself on the journey.

1. Will I grieve or mourn this loss?

2. Will I befriend my feelings of loss, or will I inhibit them?

3. Will I be a passive witness or an active participant in my grief?

4. Will I embrace the uniqueness of my grief?

5. Will I work on the six needs of mourning, or will I fall victim to the cliché "time heals all wounds?"

6. Will I believe I must achieve resolution, or will I work toward reconciliation?

7. Will I embrace my transformation?

8. Will this loss add to my "divine spark" or will it take away my life force?

This book provides the answers that will help you clarify your experiences and encourage you to make choices that honor the transformational nature of grief and loss.

ISBN 978-1-879651-62-3 • 176 pages • softcover • $18.95

Living in the Shadow of the Ghosts of Grief
Step into the Light

Reconcile old losses and open the door to infinite joy and love

Are you depressed? Anxious? Angry? Do you have trouble with trust and intimacy? Do you feel a lack of meaning and purpose in your life? You may well be Living in the Shadow of the Ghosts of Grief.

When you suffer a loss of any kind—whether through abuse, divorce, job loss, the death of someone loved or other transitions, you naturally grieve inside. To heal your grief, you must express it. That is, you must mourn your grief. If you don't, you will carry your grief into your future, and it will undermine your happiness for the rest of your life.

This compassionate guide will help you learn to identify and mourn your carried grief so you can go on to live the joyful, whole life you deserve.

ISBN 978-1-879651-51-7 • 160 pages • softcover • $13.95

Praise for Living in the Shadow of the Ghosts of Grief

"For all of you who have had losses but never had the opportunity to mourn, this is the book for you. Dr. Wolfelt gently and with warmth helps you understand that it is never too late to do what he calls catch-up mourning. Alan Wolfelt is a master at helping us understand ourselves and others."— Penny Hull

"All counselors should read this captivating, clear, compassionate and informed book. It has powerful applicability for therapists who work with people impacted by life losses. I have purchased more than 25 copies and gifted them to my family, friends, and colleagues."
— T. Crean

To contact Dr. Wolfelt about speaking engagements or training opportunities at his Center for Loss and Life Transition, email him at DrWolfelt@centerforloss.com.